Authentic Antarctica

Leading With Purpose

Anna Frebel

www.annafrebel.com

Leading With Purpose

In November 2023, I spent 20 amazing days voyaging to Antarctica with the global leadership initiative, *Homeward Bound*. Together with 108 other women and non-binary people with a STEM background, we participated in an immersive leadership training to challenge ourselves, and to learn about our planet and how we can collectively create a more sustainable future for us all.

Why Antarctica, you ask? Well, it's more than just a beautiful place. It's a unique location on Earth that facilitates self-discovery and learning about your core values. Without the usual distractions, Antarctica is an invitation to figure out what kind of leader you want to be. Antarctica is an invitation to practice leadership. Because leadership *is* a practice, not a person. It's a mindset, it's a lifestyle. And yes, it is also a place to meet adorable penguins!

This book collects my photographic images of the stunning beauty of Antarctica, along with my reflections and insights from going through the leadership training on the ship.

What I learned to appreciate is that leadership is about being intentional. It's about how we want to show up in this world every single day. Stepping into a leadership role is about the choices we make, and how we choose to show up – every moment, every day, and every situation, for ourselves and for others.

As a leadership program founder and instructor myself, I now teach that life is not just about what you do, but about who we want to be when we are in charge. The truth is, we can only *do* once we know who we *are*. Any choices we will ever make critically depend on who we are as a person and as a leader.

This book is my invitation to you: Learn about Antarctica and its role for the planet, explore who you want to be, and practice your leadership. Everyone is leading something – your family, at work, and in your community – and start creating the life you want for yourself and those around you.

Anna Frebel, January 2025

Content

Discover Antarctica

An Overview

Antarctic Treaty

The Antarctic Treaty remains one of the most enduring and successful examples of international cooperation, showing how nations can come together to protect a shared global resource and prevent geopolitical tensions in one of the most remote regions on Earth – Antarctica.

On December 1, 1959, the Antarctic Treaty was signed by twelve countries: the United States, the Soviet Union, the United Kingdom, Argentina, Australia, Chile, France, New Zealand, Norway, South Africa, Belgium, and Japan.

The treaty was driven by the desire to ensure that Antarctica would not become a point of international conflict, and to promote peaceful cooperation in scientific research, and its environmental protection.

By now, 57 countries have signed it.

The treaty established these principles:

Peaceful Purposes:
Antarctica shall be used for peaceful purposes only; it was designated a zone free from armed conflict. Nuclear explosions and disposal of radioactive waste were banned.

Scientific Freedom and Collaboration:
All countries shall have the right to conduct research in Antarctica. Research shall be through cooperation, exchange and collaboration rather than competition, with results to be openly shared.

Suspension of Territorial Claims:
During the treaty's duration, collective stewardship shall govern Antarctica rather than any sovereignty claims. Existing territorial claims were frozen and new claims prohibited.

Environmental Protection:
The treaty paved the way for protecting Antarctica's delicate ecosystem, such as the Environmental Protocol (1991) which established strict environmental standards.

Inspections and Transparency:
To maintain trust among signatories for all to uphold the peaceful and scientific purposes of the treaty, operations shall be transparent and allow on-site inspections.

The Icy Continent

Weddell Sea

Antarctic Peninsula

Ronne Ice Shelf

South Pole

East Antarctica

West Antarctica

Ross Ice Shelf

Ross Sea

Southern Ocean

3

Off to Antarctica

Chile

Argentina

Porto Madryn

Falkland Islands

Stanley

Tierra Del Fuego

Ushuaia

Cape Horn

Drake Passage

Southern Ocean

South Shetland Is

Walker Bay

Melchior Is

Anvers Is

Livingston Is

Aitcho Is

Elephant Is

Palmer Station

Spert Is

Deception Is

Antarctic Peninsula

Iceberg Alley

Orne Habour

Joinville Is

Kinnes Cove

South Georgia Is

Larsen Ice Shelf

Port Lockroy

Cuverville Is

Gerlache Strait

Grytviken

Gentoo

Sleepy Gentoo

Curious Gentoo

Penguins
Overview

King penguin mom

Sleepy
Chinstrap

Busy
Chinstrap

Chinstrap

King penguin dad

Moulting King chick

Adélie

Happy Adélie

Fluffy Adélie

Lego
penguin

Magellanic

Cheeky Magellanic

Rockhopper

Rockhopper yogi

5

King Penguins

"Rough day" King chick

Moulting King chick

King penguin mom

King penguin

King penguins are the second-largest penguin species after the Emperor penguins, standing 35-37 inches tall and weighing 20 to 30 pounds. Their regal appearance, with vibrant orange and gold markings around the neck, head and beak, makes them easily identifiable.

These penguins are very gregarious and breed in large colonies on subantarctic islands, including the Falkland Islands. Unlike most penguins, King penguins do not build nests but incubate their eggs on their feet. They breed every other year, as their offspring only go to sea at about one year of age. King penguins are expert divers, capable of reaching depths of over 1,000 feet while foraging for lantern fish and squid.

Magellanic Penguins

Splashy Magellanic

Magellanic penguin

Magellanic runner

Cheeky Magellanic

Magellanic penguins are medium-sized, reaching about 24 inches in height and weighing between 8 and 14 pounds. These penguins showcase an all black-and-white plumage, with a black beak, gray feet, and a distinctive set of black bands across their chest.

Native to the Southern coasts of South America, particularly Argentina, Chile, and the Falkland Islands, they prefer to nest in burrows to shield themselves from harsh weather and predators.

Magellanic penguins are known for their long migrations, often traveling thousands of miles between breeding and feeding grounds.

Rockhopper Penguins

Southern Rockhopper
penguin

Rockhopper mom

Rockhopper Queen

Rockhopper yogi

Southern Rockhopper penguins are smaller, standing about 20 inches tall and weighing 5 to 9 pounds. Easily identified by their bright yellow-orange crest feathers and distinctive red eyes, these penguins are known for their lively behavior and for hopping over rocks and jumping up steep cliffs in their rugged island habitats.

They are found on subantarctic islands, such as the Falkland Islands, South Georgia, and the Kerguelen Islands. Southern Rockhoppers can dive up to 300 feet deep and feed primarily on crustaceans, small fish and squid.

Gentoo Penguins

Mama Gentoo

Gentoo in a hurry

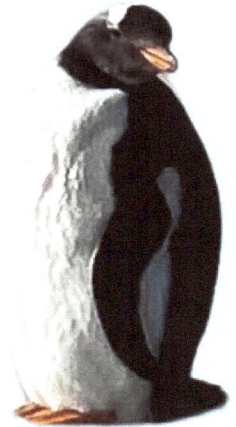

Sleepy Gentoo

Gentoo penguins are medium-sized, growing to about 30 inches in height and weighing between 8 and 12 pounds. Their appearance includes a white head stripe, white belly, bright orange feet, and a red-orange beak.

Native to subantarctic regions and the Antarctic Peninsula, Gentoo penguins are highly social and form large colonies. They build nests from pebbles and sticks (when available) and share the duties of incubating two eggs and caring for chicks. Known for their speed, they are the fastest swimming penguin species, reaching speeds of up to 22 miles per hour.

Curious Gentoo

Adélie Penguins

Happy Adélie

Fluffy Adélie

Porpoising Adélie

Adélie penguins are one of the smaller penguin species, standing about 27 inches tall and weighing around 8 to 9 pounds. Easily recognized by their all black heads, white bellies, and distinctive white rings around their black eyes, they are found all along the Antarctic coastline where they thrive in the colder climate.

Adélie penguins build nest of pebbles on sloped hills, with both males and females sharing the duties of egg incubation and chick-rearing. They are well-adapted to the extreme cold of Antarctica and primarily feed on krill and small fish.

Adélie penguin

Chinstrap Penguins

Busy Chinstrap

Sleepy Chinstrap

Hungry Chinstrap

Chinstrap penguins are relatively small, standing at about 28 inches tall and weighing around 7 to 9 pounds. They are named for the thin black band under their chins, which resembles a helmet strap. They have black beaks and rose-colored feet

Chinstraps are found in large colonies across the Southern Ocean, from the Antarctic Peninsula to subantarctic islands. They are known for their energetic and sometimes combative nature. They feed mainly on krill and fish, with both parents playing active roles in in curation and chick-rearing.

Chinstrap penguin

Icebergs

Floating ice and icebergs are found in the ocean close to Antarctica. They are categorized according to their sizes and shapes.

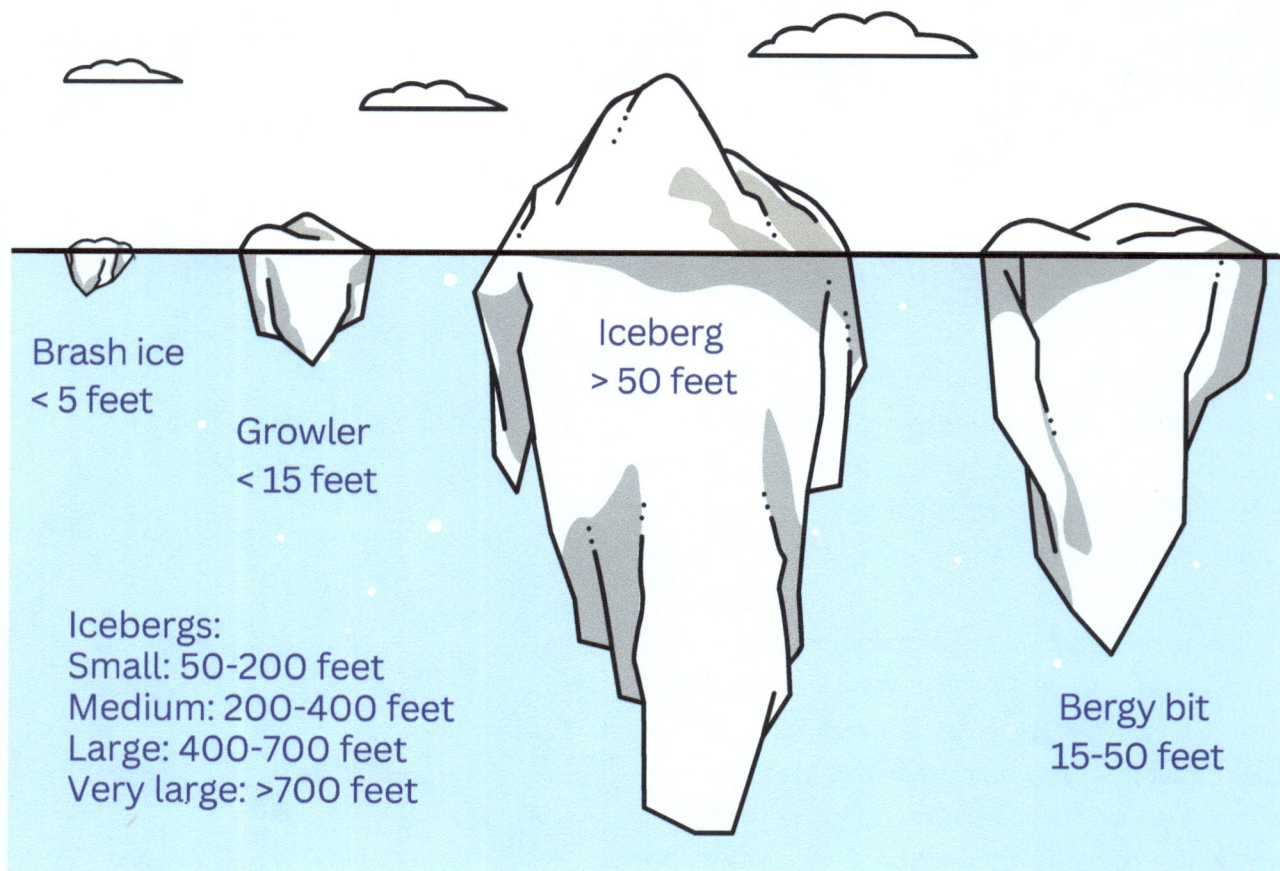

Brash ice
< 5 feet

Growler
< 15 feet

Iceberg
> 50 feet

Bergy bit
15-50 feet

Icebergs:
Small: 50-200 feet
Medium: 200-400 feet
Large: 400-700 feet
Very large: >700 feet

Icebergs

Tabular iceberg

Blocky iceberg

Wedged iceberg

Dome iceberg

Pinnacle iceberg

Dry dock iceberg

The shape of an iceberg tells about its history and origin.

Tabular icebergs are broken-off ice sheets. Blocky and wedges are much smaller versions of tabular icebergs.

Iceberg with smooth tops have recently toppled over. Some have dome-like shapes. As the iceberg's bottom slowly melts in the saltwater, it eventually topples over which reveals what is underneath, e.g. ancient blue ice.

Icebergs with rugged edges are still "as is", as they were when they broke off.

Pinnacle icebergs have bizarre shapes and pointy spires. Dry dock icebergs also have a water channel going through the middle.

A previous water line can often be observed for smaller icebergs, bergy bits and growlers, showing that what previously laid beneath the surface.

Glaciers

How Are Glaciers Made?

Glaciers are formed over long periods of time through a fascinating process that begins with snow. Each winter, snow accumulates, layer by layer. As time passes, the weight of new snowfall compresses the layers beneath, gradually turning fluffy, light snow into dense, solid ice.

This process takes years, centuries, and even millennia. With each successive layer, the snow becomes harder and more compact, squeezing out the air pockets within. Eventually, the glacier is fully build up this way. Icebergs originate when ice breaks off a glacier and fall into the ocean.

Why is Glacial Ice Blue?

Glacial ice often appears blue, which might seem surprising given that we usually associate ice with being white. The reason behind this blue color lies in the structure of the ice. Fresh snow, which is contains countless tiny air bubbles, reflects all colors of light, giving it a white appearance. However, once the snow has compacted into glacial ice, the air bubbles are mostly squeezed out and eliminated. This compacted ice has a unique structure: It forms a hexagonal crystal lattice.

This is the same shape that many naturally occurring crystals, including the blue sapphire, take. These crystals absorb the red light with its longer wavelengths while scattering the blue light that consists of shorter wavelengths. This results in the glacier's characteristic blue hue, just like sapphire.

Ancient Blue Ice

The blue color is an indication that the ice has been compressed and compacted over thousands of years. The more compressed the ice is, the bluer it becomes, signaling that the iceberg is exceptionally old, often tens of thousands of years old.

Why is the Underwater Portion of an Iceberg Always Blue?

An iceberg's submerged portion often appears blue as well. In the water, the outer, more recent layers of the iceberg melt first, exposing progressively older ice which is bluer. In addition, the pressure and weight of the iceberg cause the underwater portion to become even denser, further compacting the crystalline structure. As a result, the blue color is visible both above and below the water's surface.

Leading With Purpose

Ten Reflections
On Growth And Transformation

1. New Beginnings

In November 2023, I traveled to Antarctica for an unforgettable three weeks of leadership training in an extreme environment. The experience was all about self-reflection and growth, planning for a more sustainable future, and, of course, plenty of penguin and wildlife watching.

I journeyed to the end of the Earth with an incredible group of 108 women and non-binary people in STEM, as part of global STEM women's leadership initiative *Homeward Bound*. Together, we learned firsthand about Antarctica, climate action, the global ocean system, and all things penguin. This transformative experience challenged us in new ways and prompted us to fact what kind of leaders we want to be – for our children, for our communities, for society, and for our planet.

The poem *For a New Beginning* by Irish poet John O'Donohue captures the deeply shared sense of purpose and renewal that developed among us on the ship and in the ice.

The final verse resonates deeply with me.

[...]
Awaken your spirit to adventure;
Hold nothing back, learn to find ease in risk;
Soon you will be home in a new rhythm,
For your soul senses the world that awaits
you.

Participating in this leadership initiative and
the Antarctic journey has helped me to
further recognize my own strengths and
potential. My new beginning quietly took
place back in Antarctica, at the bottom of
the world without fireworks or champagne.
The transformation was as silent and
profound as the monumental glaciers that
surrounded us throughout our voyage.

The *Homeward Bound* program was
designed to guide us in rethinking and
rediscovering who we are, who we want to
become, what our purpose is, and what
kinds of short and long-term actions we are
prepared to take.

We were challenged to map out our goals, both individually and collectively, from small, everyday intentions to our shared global vision for creating a more sustainable future on Earth.

Just like a massive ice sheet that has broken away finds its new form as a tabular iceberg, the rhythm of my life has shifted and taken on new shape. After nearly a year back home, I feel more grounded, more forward-looking, less distracted by small things, and my approach to leadership has become more transparent, calm, and all about the big picture. Having navigated 20 to 30 feet high waves on the ship, I now face challenges as a surfer would — by riding the wave.

My soul is eager to continue exploring this new world, filled with love, friendship, awareness, clarity, gratitude, countless penguin stories, and the many wonderful memories of this life-changing journey to the icy continent.

2. Disconnection

Do we ever disconnect these days? Shortly before our three-week voyage to Antarctica in November 2023, we had been informed to handle no internet connectivity on the ship. While the idea was daunting, I had prepared diligently for being cut off from the world.

I had downloaded the program materials and a few movies to enjoy during downtime, created video messages for my kids, prepared my students, and set up an automated email response that I would be offline for some time.

This process gave my departure far more weight than I had anticipated; at times, it felt as though I might never return. Leaving instructions, anticipating needs, and ensuring nothing was left unattended took a major effort and, at times, was exhausting.

After years of anticipation and a lot of preparation, I was finally on my way to Argentina and to meet the 108 other STEM women and non-binary people to voyage together to Antarctica. As I reached the airport, I remembered that part of the Homeward Bound leadership training is all about leading in uncertainty and learning to let things go.

Fast forward to being on our ship, the *Island Sky*. One of the first announcements was about using the onboard Starlink satellite internet. We learned that large icebergs could potentially block the incoming low-angle signal. While my inner science nerd found this fascinating, my astronomy brain couldn't ignore the irony.

The Starlink satellites enabling internet in remote locations, including Antarctica, are the same ones causing major issues for astronomy and the discovery of the cosmos. Brightly reflecting sunlight, swarms of satellites are visible in the night sky and in astronomical images. This significantly impacts data collection and scientific research. The satellites are permanently altering our night sky and humanity's ability to explore it.

So there I was, holding the card with the access code. It ended up in the bedside table drawer. Days later, I realized that all my trip preparations had somehow created a mental space for me to let go of the need to always check email, social media, and everything else online. Surprisingly, I was perfectly fine not knowing what my inbox looked like.

About halfway through the trip, however, a sense of obligation surfaced. I reluctantly tried to check my work email "just to see."

But thanks to two-factor authentication and no phone service, this urge instantly resolved and access to my inbox was prevented for the entire duration of my trip. It was glorious to just disconnect, and instead connect with wonderful people and penguins.

I ended up using the onboard internet in the second half of the trip, to connect with family. I posted a few things on social media and did some searches about the places we visited. A full day after disembarkation, I finally dared to reconnect with my inbox. A full day after disembarkation, I finally dared to reconnect with my inbox. But I felt just fine letting my emails wait, so I closed my laptop again. I knew that diving into the 1,000+ messages would pull me right back into everyday life – I wasn't quite ready yet.

Since then, I have struggled to keep up. I still have unread messages from that time. Since then, I have also had no issues letting my inbox grow like an untended garden needing some serious pruning. It's actually been quite liberating not to worry about it quite as much.

So, if I've ignored you over the past year, please know it's not about you; it's about my new, more "Antarctica-chill" self. Just as before we were all glued to our smartphones, you're all in my thoughts and heart, just not my fingertips. Maybe we can call or meet instead and actually connect?

3. Out Of This World

Antarctica is often said to be the closest place on Earth to another planet. Indeed, the icy continent boasts majestic snowy mountains, extreme cold and weather, and wildlife uniquely adapted to its environment — much like what one might imagine on another planet. As an astronomer, I had always been curious about interplanetary travel, and our voyage to Antarctica offered a little bit of it.

After crossing the Drake Passage, we first arrived at the South Shetland Islands near the northwestern tip of the Antarctic Peninsula where snow-covered mountains began to frame our views. The rugged, steep landscape was awe-inspiring, although from a distance it first reminded me of the French Alps.

Our very first landing on Aitcho Island was very exciting as we encountered hundreds of adorable Gentoo penguins. At the beach, they were leaping in and out of the water, fighting about rocks to impress their mates, waddling around to build their nests, and chattering loudly and proudly. It was fantastic to witness these penguins in the wild for the first time.

But it didn't quite feel like having stepped onto another planet just yet.

35

The next day, we reached nearby Deception Island, the caldera of an active volcano. Early in the morning, our ship passed through a narrow opening called Neptune's Bellows and into the water-filled crater of this volcano. A strikingly different landscape revealed itself. The geology showcased traces of past lava flows that created a dramatic, checkered terrain in black, gray, and white.

With our zodiacs, we soon landed at Telefon Bay on the far side of the caldera, at a beach made from pitch-black volcanic sand and gravel, unlike anything we had seen before. Beyond the beach stretched a massive snowfield that we were about to cross to get to a ridge to overlook the entire bay.

With all our gear — including life jackets that we wore for every landing — and the loose snow causing me to sink a foot with every step, my progress across the snowfield was slow and sweaty. I looked around to take in my surroundings. The blinding expanse of white was disorienting at first, but with each deep breath and heavy step through the crackling snow, more of the mountainous landscape began to appear. Marching along, this place suddenly felt profoundly different from what we had seen before.

Soaking up the silence, I became fully immersed in the vast and intricately styled black-and-white environment. The snow smelled fresh as it crackled beneath my boots. Each inhale was crisp and made me feel so alive, filling me with both clarity and calm. The landscape seemed to invite me to slow down, reflect, and simply be.

With each step, I felt a growing sense of gratitude for the untouched beauty surrounding me and that we must take better care of our planet if we want to preserve nature and places such as Antarctica.

The vastness of this precious landscape made me feel both small and deeply connected to place. Would it feel like this to stand on another planet? Might an icy planetary world look like this? I was traveling through the Solar System and beyond until a sudden gust of wind swiftly brought me back to Earth, making me stumble as I climbed further.

I was so present in the moment I didn't even notice that others began calling after me because I accidentally dropped a glove.

Finally, from the top of the ridge I looked all around. I could see the caldera, the surrounding mountains, valleys, cliffs, and snow-laden ridges. The view was just breathtaking. It felt like a masterful painting, yet alien in its structure and beauty — truly out of this world.

9. There Is Only Plan A

There Is Only Plan A

For the entire voyage, passengers remained on the cruise ship, but landings or zodiac cruises were scheduled each day. The landing sites for each ship are pre-scheduled months in advance through the International Association of Antarctic Tour Operators (IAATO), which operates a centralized booking system. The ship's itinerary thus reflects which places are available for a visit and when, and no two cruises are ever the same.

IAATO, established over 30 years ago, facilitates safe, environmentally responsible tourism in Antarctica. Their landing allocation system ensures that only one vessel visits a location at a time. This not only provides visitors with an undisturbed experience of Antarctica's pristine beauty but also safeguards its fragile ecosystem.

Throughout our 20-day journey, we spotted another ship on the distant horizon only three times, allowing us to feel like the only explorers in this remote world. What a privilege!

The IAATO regulations also include strict rules for protecting wildlife. Visitors must maintain at least a 15 feet distance from animals, to be kept when animals approach. To further limit disturbances, only 100 people can be ashore at a time. This may seem overly cautious, but considering the 20,000 visitors Antarctica receives during the short four-month summer season, such limitations are vital for preserving the animals' natural behavior.

Biosecurity measures were equally stringent to prevent the introduction of foreign species. Before our first landing, we carefully cleaned our jackets and gear under the expedition team's supervision. Any food, especially items such as fruit with seeds, was strictly prohibited on land.

With the avian flu having reached Antarctica, even stricter safety measures were in place. Before and after every landing, our boots were doused in Virkon, a highly potent disinfectant to protect the animals that makes Antarctica special. We could only touch the ground with the soles of our disinfected boots. No sitting, no bags on the snow, no snow angels — none of it was allowed. While it was disappointing to forgo lying in the snow and soaking in the unique sensory experience, simply standing amidst Antarctica's awe-inspiring landscapes turned out to be just fine.

The overall success of our voyage with 13 most memorable landings and zodiac cruises was also not just because "we were lucky with the weather". It was thanks to the expertise of our highly invested expedition team which IAATO experts and award-winning polar researchers with decades of experience. They worked tirelessly behind the scenes to track weather conditions and adjust our itinerary on the fly, swapping pre-scheduled sites we could not reach for others that unexpectedly became accessible.

With unpredictable ice conditions and increasingly erratic weather and wind patterns, adapting to the moment is standard practice for Antarctic expeditions. Hence, the team leader taught us that constantly adjusting plans was to be part of our experience along with a practice of accepting change with a positive attitude. After all, resilience and adaptability are key to thriving in life's unpredictable circumstances.

Indeed, in the end, our voyage through the Antarctic Peninsula barely resembled the team's original itinerary. But isn't that part of the magic?

Because when in Antarctica, there's only ever Plan A — and it will always be amazing.

And it truly was.

3. Passionate About Penguins

Passionate About Penguins

Every year, January 20th marks the day dedicated to raising awareness about penguins. These charming little creatures face numerous challenges to their continued survival across the Southern Hemisphere.

It was simply incredibly to have the chance to visit Antarctica and had the chance to meet penguins up close. It was such an amazing experience to be surrounded by these remarkable birds, watching them waddle around, dive into the water, swim around our zodiacs, and laze on ice floats as our ship passed by.

Penguins seem perfectly adapted for the harsh and rugged Antarctic environment. I kept observing groups of penguins as they passed me. An incoming group would appear mostly white — their bellies and the undersides of their wings were bright white. Their short legs and feet were covered by white snow. Only their heads sported small black patches. Overall, this made them blend quite well into the snow-covered landscape.

As the penguins got closer, I would see more and more of their backs, and gradually they would all transform into black. Against the backdrop of dark mountains mountains, they looked like small black dots waddling around, again blending in beautifully with the surroundings. At a distance, they almost disappeared into the checkered background.

Penguins in Antarctica have no aerial predators, so they can safely move up the cliffs, hills, and even mountains without fear. A few times, we spotted penguins climbing up steep, rocky slopes, patiently and step by step. In other moments, we joyfully watched them sliding down snowy hills on their bellies. From afar, we only saw their black backs — if they had not been moving, we would probably have mistaken them for small, bare rocks or not noticed them at all. Their zig-zagging motion, however, made them easy to spot.

No matter from which angle I would see the penguins, they always seemed perfectly in sync with their environment's color scheme. The only thing that changed was my perspective. I saw them either as black dots or as white figures against the backdrop of the rocky black-white terrain.

Watching them struck me as a fascinating lesson in perspective and awareness by showing me just how much the same thing can appear completely different depending on the angle from which you view it. Yet, the penguins themselves remained of course unchanged.

Indeed, context always matters enormously — and asking the kinds of questions that help you to gather more information before rushing to any conclusions. Uncovering both sides of the story, much like the penguins were either standing out from the snow or blending into the landscape, can help us understand a given situation more fully.

This highlighted the decisions we have to repeatedly face every day: Choosing to fit in or rather wanting to stand out from the crowd. It's not just a matter of our choice. It's often driven by the context and we all have to adapt to it.

Port Lockroy is a small station located on tiny Goudier Island situated in a bay of Wiencke Island in the Palmer Archipelago. Historically, the station, known as "Base A," served primarily as a British Antarctic Survey research facility, these days it is more widely known as the "Penguin Post Office". In that capacity, it serves both researchers and tourists visiting the area.

I was thrilled for the chance to visit the iconic Port Lockroy and send off the postcards I had written on the ship. Mailing a card from there felt like the ultimate proof that I had actually made it to Antarctica, to the end of the world.

Upon our arrival, the four staff members were eager to show us the site, answer questions, and guide us through the small historic Bransfield House museum about Antarctic exploration and life in Antarctica many decades ago. Then, with a special Antarctica stamp, I proudly mailed postcards to my kids and some friends, creating a unique and unforgettable souvenir. It took 4-8 weeks for the postcards to make their way from down South to destinations all around the globe.

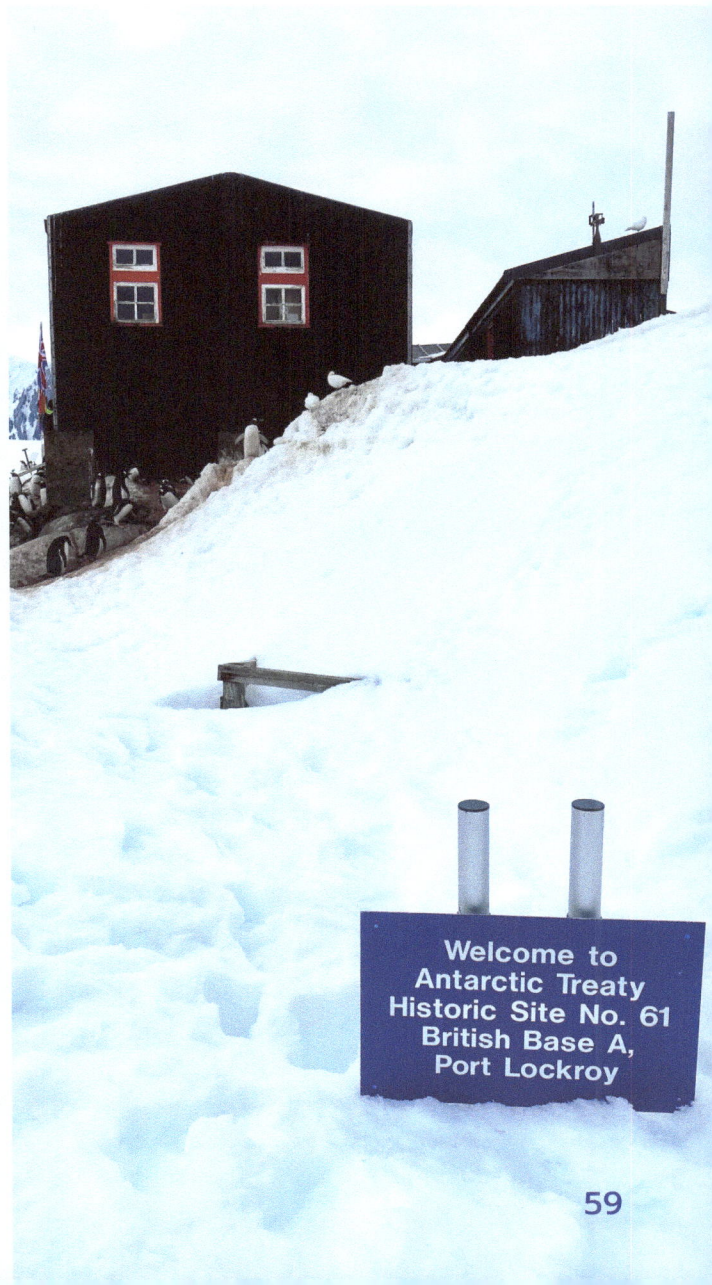

Welcome to
Antarctic Treaty
Historic Site No. 61
British Base A,
Port Lockroy

Port Lockroy was also impressive for other reasons. As we arrived in our zodiacs early that morning, we were greeted by the lively sounds and unmistakable scent of penguins.

Nestled right by the beach, the two main red-and-black historic buildings looked picture perfect against the snowy bay framed by huge glaciers. It quickly became clear that the penguins had taken over the area — much to our delight. Indeed, the historic buildings appeared to be very popular. As such, they were perched in the middle of extended guano spots. Penguins were definitely the ruling party and were breeding next to and under the buildings. And everyone seemed perfectly alright with it.

This arrangement meant we had to be careful to maintain the mandatory 15 feet distance from the penguins, who were busily building nests and stealing rocks from one another in noisy squabbles right in front of us. Sometimes it felt like the penguins were putting on a show just for us, but mostly, they were far more interested in their own business than in the touristy humans.

There was one amusing moment when I placed a few of my kids' Lego penguins in the snow to photograph them. Some of the real penguins took notice and started to approach. It may have been the first time in history that a penguin spotted a Lego. I'm sure they were very impressed by my boy's creations!

That sunny morning, the Port Lockroy Bay and surrounding icy mountains were very calm, all blue, and there was no wind. Everything seemed effortlessly beautiful and the atmosphere was immensely serene and harmonious.

While each zodiac group's visit had only been about 30 minutes, I could have spent hours there, just watching penguins swim, jumping over rocks, playing and chattering with each other to ring in the new day. Despite the constant activity of perhaps a hundred penguins all around us, everything felt just so right and perfectly in place.

During the last few precious minutes before our departure, it felt like my heart and soul became one with this most beautiful place. The countless efforts it had taken for me to go on this unusual voyage were undoubtedly worth it.

These unforgettable moments full of gratitude will nourish and inspire me for a long time.

6. Lego Penguins

A few days before my departure to Antarctica, I playfully asked my then 5 and 9-year-old boys if they wanted to build Lego penguins for me to take along. I didn't expect much, but about half an hour later, my 5-year-old walked into the kitchen, where I was making dinner. He was proudly holding something up over his head. "Mama, look, here is my penguin," he said, beaming with joy. It was a small creation of blue, white, and black Lego pieces, and it actually looked like a penguin! I was amazed at how quickly and creatively he had assembled something so recognizable from just a few bricks.

Soon after, my 9-year-old joined the fun, presenting me with a little gray Lego penguin complete with an egg under its care. Their enthusiasm melted my heart. When I asked if there was anything they wanted me to bring back from the trip, of course they asked for a real-life penguin. After some debate, we all agreed that our bathtub wasn't quite big enough to host a penguin who would want to swim around.

Instead of bringing home a new pet, I returned with something else: An adventure story featuring their very own Lego penguins.

After carefully disinfecting them to protect Antarctica's pristine environment, I brought their creations along on my zodiac trips and snapped pictures along with some real penguins. At Port Lockroy — Antarctica's post office on Goudier Island — a few Gentoo penguins came waddling by, curious about what I was up to as I was taking photos of them and those little guys. However, at Orne Harbour on continental Antarctica, the ever-so-chill Chinstrap penguins sitting on the rocks at the top of the steep ridge we all had climbed for the stunning views couldn't have cared less about me or their Lego cousins.

When I showed my boys the photos of the trip, they were thrilled! The pictures and stories greatly sparked their curiosity, leading us to learn more about different penguin species and all sorts of facts about Antarctica. I even visited my 9-year-old's class before the holidays to share what I had learned. A visit with my kindergartener's afterschool program followed soon after.

My Antarctica presentation and in-class activities about penguins ended up taking 90 minutes, with all kids highly engaged. We covered topics such as how Antarctica impacts the rest of the planet, all about icebergs, the lives of penguins and other wildlife, and ways of how to protect the icy continent's unique and fragile ecosystem with sustainable actions at home.

On the voyage, I also purchased an "Adopt-A-Penguin" package in the Falkland Islands for my boys which we visited on our way from Argentina to the Antarctic Peninsula. This Falkland program supports King penguin conservation efforts and felt like the next best thing to having a penguin of our own. We got to name "our" King penguin, and when I called the boys from the ship to share the news, they chattered with joy like penguins and instantly decided on a name. Since then, somewhere in the Falkland Islands waddles a King penguin called "Sigma Frebel" :)

7. Antarctic Sunsets

Antarctic Sunsets

In Antarctica, sunsets are of unparalleled intensity. Due to its Southern location, Antarctica experiences very distinct seasons. During winter, the Sun never rises above the horizon. But in summer, which spans from late November to early February, the icy continent is bathed in daylight. This is the season of the remarkable midnight Sun, when the Sun doesn't set for weeks. Before and after this period, in early and late summer, prolonged sunsets are a stunning feature instead.

We traveled for most of November when sunsets occurred around 11 pm, followed by two to three hours of twilight and darkness before the sun would rise again. As the Sun slowly sank, we were treated to several gorgeous sunsets. The water, dotted with countless icebergs, the frozen landscapes, and the rugged snow-covered mountains around us — everything would take on a warm glow, from golden to soft orange and pink, to fiery red and purple.

Walking around the ship during these late hours felt as though I had been transported into a painting or a fairytale. The piercing air amplified the sense of being in a completely different world. The landscape transformed into a colorful dreamscape, almost unreal in the best possible way. The intense hues, the long shadows, the calm, glistening water against the icy backdrop — Antarctica revealed its most precious and delightful side in those moments.

More than once, fire and ice were meeting in the distance, with huge beams of sunlight dramatically pointing all over the sky as the Sun was finally setting. The icebergs around us would appear in all sorts of colors, with the orange and purple ones looking the most impressive.

For me, being outside in the fresh air for expended periods of time became a time of reflection and finding clarity in between the ice. By the end of our voyage, there had been many such moments when my soul had deeply connected with this extraordinary place, leaving my heart touched forever.

More than once, while caught in the glow of those colors and the grand silence of the ice and water, we observed pairs of humpback whales peacefully swimming and playing in the distance. Their spouts sent steamy fountains into the air, making them easily identifiable. The tiny water droplets suspended in the air would often glow bright orange in the twilight, even a few minutes after the whales had dived again.

Watching the whales in this beautiful, harmonious environment reminded me time and again that we were just guests in another world — a world we must respect and fight to preserve. We must keep Antarctica cold, pristine, and magnificent. Antarctica without ice would mark an unimaginable tragedy and cause the rest of world the most severe problems. Sadly, the warming up is already happening, more and more, and in ways that are already irreversible.

8. Humpback Whales

Humpback Whales

Besides penguins, seals, and birds, which are relatively easy to encounter, Antarctica offers one more incredible animal to look out for: whales. The most common are humpback whales, but lucky onlookers may also spot orcas or other whale species. It is harder to plan for whale sightings, though, as they appear unexpectedly and on their own terms. The good news is that, sooner or later, some usually make an appearance. In fact, certain straits and areas have speed limits in place to help prevent ships from accidentally hitting whales, as these regions are known feeding grounds for them.

During our voyage through the islands of the Antarctic Peninsula, we were fortunate enough to encounter humpback whales several times. One late evening, as the summer twilight settled in, we passed through a relatively narrow strait surrounded by snow-covered mountains that had turned into shades of orange and pink in the fading light. Pairs of whales began to appear a few hundred yards away from the ship, almost as if they were basking in the last rays of the day.

It was a magical moment that was filled with color and clarity. The whales were frolicking in the calm blue water, framed by glistening icebergs and majestic mountains. This went on for more than an hour, with at least five or six pairs of whales making an appearance. They seemed to playfully interact, repeatedly blowing water into the air as they exhaled before diving, showing us their flukes, again and again. Typically, their flukes typically only emerge when they are about to deep dive but these whales kept coming back up to play.

On another occasion, a humpback whale was lunge-feeding relatively close to the ship. It kept showing us its back before repeatedly taking shallow dives. While feeding, the whale came up from beneath the surface, head held high, mouth wide open, skillfully filtering out krill and small fish through its baleen plates. Then, it would dive down again for the next round.

Compared to their massive body sizes, which can reach lengths of 40 to 50 feet, Humpback whales have relatively small dorsal fins. Hence, it's easy to miss just how large these animals are when all you get to see is a small dorsal fin at a distance. But occasionally, I could hear the water splashing as a whale resurfaced or when it exhaled to send mist and spray into the clear Antarctic air through its blowhole.

The process of feeding and diving was fast-paced and challenging to capture with my camera. When I looked at the photos later, I got a much closer look at this particular whale. It displayed the characteristic "knobs" on the upper side of its mouth, which also serve as a kind of lid for the massive bottom portion of its mouth. That bottom part was densely covered with barnacles, a sign that this was an older humpback whale who had been around for a while.

What a privilege to witness such an extraordinary creature in its natural habitat. The health of whales depends largely on the availability of krill. In turn, krill strongly rely on the Antarctic current system to thrive in the cold surface waters of the Southern Ocean.

Thinking about this interconnectedness between some of the smallest and largest animals on Earth up close was an unforgettable experience. And yet another reason as to why we must take action to slow down climate change, to preserve these unique environments, and to protect all of the diverse life present on our planet.

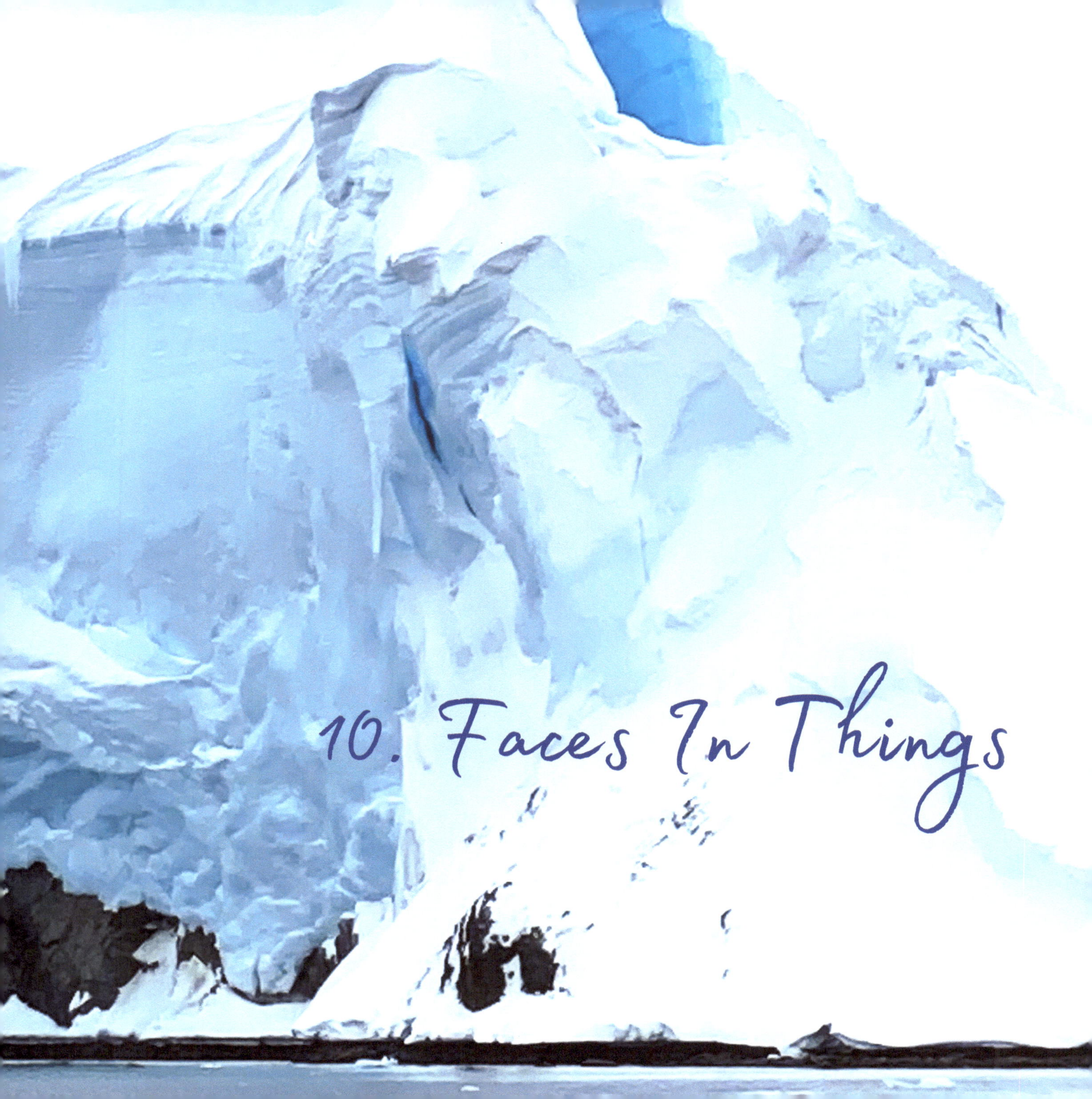

10. Faces In Things

During our voyage around the Antarctic Peninsula, we used zodiac boats to get from the ship to beaches and landing sites, exploring various islands and the Antarctic continent itself. However, landings weren't always possible due to ice conditions or the lack of suitable landing sites. In those cases, we went on 60 to 90 minute zodiac cruises, allowing us to see the animals, icebergs, and islands from the water.

These cruises were often quite cold, as we sat still in freezing temperatures and strong winds, but they offered an incredible "big picture" view of the wonder that is Antarctica. The Melchior Islands archipelago featured narrow passages with breathtaking snow-covered landscapes and floating ice sculptures all around us.

The towering icy mountains were majestic and peaceful. Looking up at these massive polished walls of ice filled me with awe and wonder every single time. Dark blue ice shimmered through the many deep cracks in the glaciers, revealing thousands of years of

91

history. We were gliding through a gigantic, ancient museum of perfectly preserved ice. What a true privilege!

As we rounded a corner, we headed straight towards another snow-covered glacier, this one more rugged, with deep crevasses and what looked like a large opening. Above it, the glacier's shape seemed to resemble the gentle face of a person with calm, closed eyes, a pronounced nose, and a pointy hat. It was as if she (or he?) was watching over the opening, welcoming us to this magical place.

On another day, we were passing through the Gerlache Strait, a stunning channel flanked by tall icy mountains on either side of the ship. As the evening approached, the sun cast a spectacular light show across the water. I walked around the ship, fully taking in the fresh and clean air and the beautiful palette of yellow, blue, and purple hues, when I noticed what looked like a reindeer swimming in the water. The iceberg far behind it was shaped like a flat-roofed warehouse or depot.

Christmas was just around the corner — had I maybe caught Santa on his way from the South Pole to visit children around the world?

Repeatedly seeing icebergs from the ship taught me that they take on all kinds of shapes, and as you pass them, new angles usually reveal additional forms. Icebergs are never quite what they seem at first, and that is not even considering what lies below the surface. Likewise, it is easy to jump to conclusions but perhaps it should not be done too quickly – nobody walks in someone else's shoes after all.

Instead, it is worth realizing that when we are able to shift our own position even just a little bit it can bring on an entirely new view. And when you shift and you start seeing reindeer in the Antarctic Ocean, it's alright to laugh, too.

So go outside and explore nature, wherever you are. There are always at least some clouds in the sky whose shapes can spark a moment of imagination. Look around for something that resonates with you, because there is always something new to discover with a fresh way of looking at things.

You may be surprised by what you find and how simply noticing something as little as a silly shape around you can make your day. And even entirely change your perspective.

Experiencing Antarctica will change how you see the world.

Photography & Locations

All photography was taken on location by Anna Frebel.

1. New Beginnings:
Melchior Islands; Kinnes Cove, Joinville Island; Gerlache Strait; Aitcho Island; Orne Harbor, continental Antarctica; Walker Bay, Livingston Island; Spert Island; portrait on page 22 taken by Karen Alexander

2. Disconnection:
Kinnes Cove, Joinville Island; Wienke Island; Spert Island; Melchior Islands; Walker Bay, Livingston Island

3. Passionate About Penguins:
Cuverville Island; Kinnes Cove, Joinville Island; Goudier Island; Orne Habor, continental Antarctica

4. Out Of This World:
Telefon Bay, Deception Island

5. Antarctica's Post Office:
Base A, Port Lockroy, Goudier Island; Wienke Island

6. Lego Penguins:
Base A, Port Lockroy, Goudier Island; Orne Habor, continental Antarctica; Cuverville Island

7. Antarctic Sunsets:
Gerlache Strait

8. Humpback Whale Tales:
Gerlache Strait; at sea

9. There Is Only Plan A:
Telefon Bay, Deception Island; Orne Harbor, continental Antarctica; Melchior Islands; at sea; Kinnes Cove, Joinville Island

10. Faces In Things:
Melchior Islands; at sea; Gerlache Strait

Acknowledgements

My journey to Antarctica has been nothing short of extraordinary, and I am deeply grateful to all who helped make this trip a reality. First and foremost, I would like to extend my heartfelt thanks to my sponsors and supporters, including my family, friends and my two boys. Your support meant the world to me!

I am immensely grateful to all the experienced *Homeward Bound* faculty who thoughtfully guided us through the extensive program. You taught us how to ask the hard questions, to face our fears, and to experience Antarctica in the most meaningful way. Thank you for the work that you do!

A very special thanks to our Antarctic expedition team, led by Claudia, Kim, Mark, Cat and others – your expert knowledge, guidance, and unwavering commitment were deeply inspiring. You made this adventure not just safe, but truly transformative.

To my HB sisters, thank you for your care, collaboration and shared enthusiasm. I greatly enjoyed connecting with you, supporting each other, and being supported as we questioned who we want to be as leaders, individually as well as collectively. Each of you brought something unique to this shared experience, and it was a true pleasure to explore magnificent Antarctica with such a diverse and passionate group.

I would also like to express my gratitude to the *Island Sky* ship captain and crew. Your skill and professionalism, especially navigating through storms and ice water ensured our safety and comfort throughout the voyage.

Thank you, Antarctica, for welcoming us with your untamed spirit. I am incredibly grateful to have had the privilege of visiting. You will stay in my heart going forward!

About The Author

Anna Frebel is an astrophysicist and full professor of physics at the Massachusetts Institute of Technology in Cambridge, MA, USA. She studies the oldest, 13 billion year old stars in the universe to learn about the cosmic origins of the chemical elements, and the formation of the Milky Way Galaxy. Besides having authored more than 180 journal articles, she has written about her galactic explorations in a popular science book, "Searching for the Oldest Stars – Ancient Relics from the Early Universe" (Princeton University Press).

In 2020, Frebel co-founded the *Leadership and Professional Strategies and Skills* (LEAPS) program for MIT graduate students and postdocs in STEM fields, which won the 2023 Irwin Sizer Award for "Most Significant Improvement to MIT Education." She serves as an instructor with MIT Professional Education, teaching leadership courses for women.

For more than 15 years, she has mentored and advised students, postdocs and junior faculty, and helped them chart their successful STEM careers. Frebel has tirelessly advocated for access to leadership and professional development training for all career stages across MIT and elsewhere. Programs such as LEAPS also play their part in creating a more inclusive and equitable workplace climate so that everyone can reach their full potential.

Frebel is a member of the global women's leadership initiative *Homeward Bound* which took her to Antarctica in 2023 for three weeks of intensive in-person leadership training along with 108 other women and non-binary people with a STEM background.

www.ingramcontent.com/pod-product-compliance
Lightning Source LLC
Chambersburg PA
CBHW060809270326
41928CB00002B/31